CHAMPIONSHIP

BASEBALL

BY RON FRASER

Published By:
The Athletic Institute
200 Castlewood Drive
North Palm Beach, FL 33408
U.S.A.

Cover Photo by
Richard C. Lewis

Photography by
Frank Morris
Vincent Pecorella

Demonstrators
University of Miami Hurricanes

Library of Congress Catalog Card Number 83-70383
ISBN 0-87670-089-X

A Word from Publisher

THIS SPORTS PUBLICATION, is but one item in a comprehensive list of sports instructional aids, such as video cassettes, 16mm films, 8mm silent loops and filmstrips which are made available by The Athletic Institute. This book is part of a master plan which seeks to make the benefits of athletics, physical education and recreation available to everyone.

The Athletic Institute is a not-for-profit organization devoted to the advancement of athletics, physical education and recreation. The Institute believes that participation in athletics and recreation has benefits of inestimable value to the individual and to the community.

The nature and scope of the many Institute programs are determined by a Professional Advisory Committee, whose members are noted for their outstanding knowledge, experience and ability in the fields of athletics, physical education and recreation.

The Institute believes that through this book the reader will become a better performer, skilled in the fundamentals of this fine event. Knowledge and the practice necessary to mold knowledge into playing ability are the keys to real enjoyment in playing any game or sport.

Howard J. Bruns
President and Chief Executive Officer
The Athletic Institute

D. E. Bushore
Executive Director
The Athletic Institute

Preface

This book should provide young players and coaches with the necessary fundamentals to develop the basic baseball skills. These basics should be practiced for as long as one plays the game. My philosophy/success at the University of Miami for the last 20 years has been based on teaching fundamentals and then constantly practicing them. One mistake made by many coaches is in assuming that players know what to do.

Baseball is a game of mistakes. Like any other team sport, baseball is a game where the winner made fewer mistakes. Therefore, my coaching philosophy has been to have a sound fundamental team developed by practice, practice and more practice, and to force the other team into making mistakes by being aggressive and also by playing percentage baseball.

A coach can develop a good defensive ballclub, aggressive base runners and produce pitchers who can throw strikes. This theory can win games for you, especially at the high school level and in lower classifications of baseball. Hitting is something much harder to develop, but in stressing certain fundamentals, your hitters can be taught to make contact with the ball and force the other team to make all the plays defensively. Great hitters and proven hitters are a plus, but do not come along that often.

It is the intention of this book to help young people to understand the concept of the sport so that they will have more fun playing the greatest game on earth.

— Ron Fraser

Table of Contents

Throwing and
Catching the Ball

Throwing a Baseball

Throwing is basic to all baseball. The mechanics can be described in terms of the grip and the arm and body action. A player must use his entire body to make throws with strength and accuracy.

The Grip

The proper grip should be used for every throw. Grip the ball across the seams so that the flight of the ball will be straight to the target without curving or sailing. Grip the ball with index and middle fingers on top and about three-quarters of an inch apart. The thumb should be directly under the index finger. The ball should be held firm and secure but not so tightly that it will be forced into the heal of the hand and smothered, preventing good wrist action.

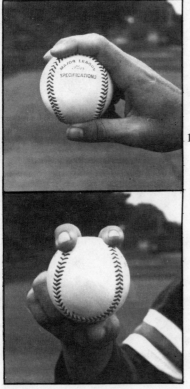

1. Consistently grip ball with index and middle fingers slightly spread with thumb under index finger.

2. Remaining fingers are bent or curled slightly to side and relaxed.

Arm and Body Motion

After gripping the ball correctly, the body should make a half turn away from the direction the ball is to be thrown. The rear, or pivot, foot must also be turned away to a 90 degree angle from the target so that the player can rotate his hips and make a firm push-off for power.

The Crow Hop

The basic overhand throw should be used by outfielders all the time and by infielders whenever possible.

On most throws, a player must learn to use the crow hop. This is a short hop used to shift body weight to get more power behind the throw. It also eliminates the tendency of the player throwing with just his arm.

The arm is extended behind the body with elbow bent and wrist cocked. While swinging the arm forward, the weight is shifted to the front leg. Pivot on the front foot, lead with the elbow and uncock the wrist with a snapping motion to release the ball slightly above and in front of the head. Follow through with the throwing hand aimed at target, swinging back leg around for better balance and to get into a ready position.

1. Extend arm behind body with elbow bent and wrist cocked.

2. Shift weight to front leg while swinging through arm forward, leading with elbow.

3. Pivot on front foot, extend arm and uncock wrist with a snapping motion to release ball slightly above and in front of head.

4. Follow through with throwing hand pointing toward target.
5. Swing back leg around into balanced, ready position.

The Sidearm and Underhand Throws

There are some situations where a player simply must grab the ball and throw without taking the time to grip it correctly. Such sidearm and underhand throws should only be used when a player has to make a quick throw. Sidearm and underhand throws are more difficult to control because the ball has a tendency to slide or sink. In making these throws, the fielder does not have time to straighten to a full, upright position before making the play. The body action is abbreviated to save time, putting more stress on the throwing arm.

5

In executing the sidearm throw, swing the arm out from the shoulder and around, parallel to the ground.

A quick layback, whiplike motion of the arm and snap of the wrist are essential elements of the underhand throw.

In either case, a good follow through is always important.

1. Abbreviated body action saves time but puts more stress on throwing arm.
2. In sidearm throw, arm stays parallel to ground.

3. With underhand throw, arm has whiplike motion with wrist snap.

Catching a Baseball

The position of the glove when catching a baseball depends on whether the throw is above the waist or below.

Generally, the fingers of the glove point up when catching a ball above the waist and point downward when making a catch below the waist. For a catch at belt level, the fingers point more outward from the body than either up or down.

Catch the ball with both arms relaxed and extended toward the ball. As the ball is caught, the elbows bend to absorb the force of the throw. Catching the ball with a stiff arm results in a sore catching hand.

Cover the ball with the throwing hand as soon as the ball enters the glove to make sure the ball doesn't pop out and to throw quickly if necessary.

1. Glove fingers up when catching ball above waist.

2. Fingers down when catching below the waist and somewhat outward when making catch at belt level.

3. Bend elbows to absorb force of ball.
4. Cover ball with throwing hand to secure ball and to make quick throw if necessary.

Fielding

Ready Position

As a fielder, always assume that the ball will be hit to you. Think through in advance what you will do with the ball once you get it.

Assume a ready position so that when the ball is delivered to the batter, you move from a position of balance. This means that your weight is forward and over the balls of your feet.

Whenever you must move more than a few steps to field a ball, sprint toward the ball, then slow up to gain body control just prior to fielding the ball. Too often fielders move slowly at first, then accelerate when attempting to field the ball. Oftentimes errors are the result of this type of play.

1. Ready Position: Face batter, feet comfortably spread, knees bent, weight forward on balls of feet, and eyes fixed on action.
2. Assume ball will be hit to you.
3. Anticipate what to do with ball.
4. Move quickly and decisively from a balanced, ready position.

Fielding Ground Balls in the Infield

Whenever possible, ground balls should be fielded in the middle of the body. Carry the glove close to the ground with fingers pointing downward. Bend at the waist to get your head in position to follow the ball with your eyes.

With the glove just off the ground surface, the arms are relaxed and extended in front of the body. The head must stay down to follow the ball into the glove with your eyes.

Glove the ball with elbows in front of your knees. Secure the ball with your throwing hand and begin throwing motion.

Again, the type of throw depends upon how much time you have to make the play. Whenever possible, use a full arm and body motion preceded by a skip and step toward the target. To throw more quickly or toss to a teammate close by, the sidearm or underhand throw may be used, eliminating the skip and step.

1. Field ball in middle of body when possible.
2. Bend at waist to get head in position to follow ball with eyes.

3. Carry glove slightly above ground surface. Keep head down. Extend arms in front of body.
4. Glove ball with elbows in front of knees. Follow ball into glove with eyes.

5. Secure ball with throwing hand. Make overhead, sidearm or underhand throw as time permits and situation requires.

Fielding a Ground Ball to Your Right or Left

Quite obviously, not all ground balls are hit directly to you. Most often they are not.

All basic fielding techniques apply when scooping up a ground ball to your right or left. Move quickly in line with the ball to field the ball in the middle of your body if possible. You may have time only to stretch for the ball.

Be sure to keep your eyes on the ball all the way, set up, then make a strong, accurate throw to the appropriate base.

TO YOUR RIGHT

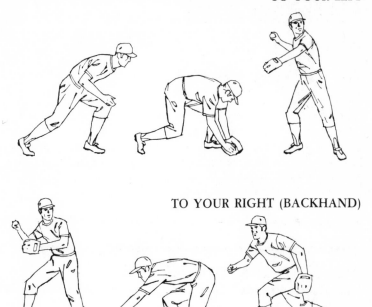

TO YOUR LEFT

TO YOUR RIGHT (BACKHAND)

Tips for Infielders

Always charge balls hit slowly or with medium speed. As the old saying goes, "Play the Ball, Don't Let the Ball Play You!" This simply means that you have two options. Charge the ball and while doing so, choose the bounce or hop to field the ball. Or, lay back and wait for the ball, taking the chance that you may have to glove the ball on a difficult, in-between hop or that the ball might take an erratic bounce over your head.

Keep the ball in front of you. It is impossible to field ground balls cleanly every time. However, the hustling ball player very often avoids an error by scrambling after the ball to throw the runner out.

By knocking the ball down and keeping it in front, you stand a good chance of making the putout with a quick recovery and throw. Once the ball gets past you, the chances of your recovering in time to throw the runner out are considerably less.

Keep your eyes on the ball. Often, in anticipation of making the throw, an infielder will take his eye off the ball at the last instant. Invariably in such a case, the ball skips under or over the glove. Keep your head down and "look" the ball into your glove.

Take time to set up before throwing. After ranging far to your left or right to field a ball, you may feel that you have to get rid of the ball quickly and rightly so. It takes just another instant to plant then brace the rear leg for the throw to the base. By doing so, the chances are much less of your throwing the ball three rows up in the grandstand.

Fielding a Ground Ball in the Outfield

The tactics of fielding a ground ball in the outfield vary with the game situation although the basic techniques are the same as when fielding a ground ball in the infield.

Ground Ball Hit Sharply with Nobody on Base

Sprint to the ball then slow speed when within three strides of the ball. Drop one knee to the ground to block the ball should it elude your glove.

Base Hit with Runners on Base

Charge the ball thens low up to field the ball as an infielder would in the infield. Bend at the waist, extend your arms and keep your eyes on the ball.

Hit with Winning Run in Scoring Position

Sprint to the ball without slowing up. Field the ball to the glove side of the body rather than in front to avoid kicking the ball. Obviously, with the runner in scoring position this is an all-or-nothing type play.

Throw to Infield

In all cases, step and throw with a full, overhand arm motion, placing backspin on the ball so that the trajectory will hold true.

Pull the opposite hip and shoulder down to bring the throwing arm more overhand, thereby adding greater body action to the throw.

Practice long throws to second, third and home plate. Make throws so as to bounce once before reaching the base. Also practice throwing on the fly to the glove side of a relay man. Throw to hit a cut-off man on the fly as well.

1. In all cases when making throw to infield, use a full, overhand arm motion.
2. Pull opposite hip and shoulder down to get more body action into throw.

3. Practice throws to bases, one bounce to bases. Throw on the fly to relay and cut-off men. Make "level" trajectory throws to infield.

Catching a Fly Ball in the Outfield

One basic admonition underlies catching all fly balls in the outfield — **get to the ball quickly, get under it and wait.**

Turn quickly in the direction in which the ball is hit. It may take an instant to determine or "judge" the direction, speed and distance of the batted ball. Practice to make such assessments quickly and accurately.

Always check the direction and velocity of the wind. Such information is helpful in determining in which direction to turn for fly balls hit directly overhead or line drives. For an overhead fly ball, simply turn in the direction in which the wind is blowing.

1. Get to ball quickly, get under it and wait.

2. Catch ball at head or chest level with fingers pointing skyward.

3. Practice judging the direction, speed and distance of batted balls. "Shag" balls often to keep sharp.

4. Check wind direction and velocity as you take the field each inning. Wind may change during course of game.

On calm days, line drives curve toward the foul lines. A right-handed batter tends to hook the ball down the left-field foul line and slice it toward the right-field foul line. Conversely, the left-handed batter hooks the ball toward the right-field line and slices it to the left-field line. A particularly strong wind in one direction or the other may cause the ball to curve more or prevent it from curving as much.

Tips for Outfielders

Concentrate on the game and anticipate what your next play would be should the ball come to you. In some games, outfielders may get few chances to field the ball. This may be particularly true if the pitcher is a low ball pitcher with a good sinking fast ball. In such games it may be easy to "daydream" and lose contact with the game. Bear down on every pitch. Don't be caught napping.

To catch balls hit over your head, run with your back to the infield and turn your head to watch the ball over your shoulder. In the absence of a strong cross wind in one direction or the other, turn to your glove side to run backward. Don't back pedal. Get to the ball the quickest way. If time permits turn to face the infield and make a normal catch at head or chest level with the fingers of the glove pointing skyward.

To catch sinking line drive, keep your glove to the side of the body. As you dip down to catch the ball, chances are better that you won't kick your glove to jar the ball loose if your glove is out to the side rather than in front.

As an outfielder, call an infielder off a ball which you can catch. Your momentum carries you toward the infield whereas his momentum carries him away.

Also, to avoid colliding with fellow outfielders or infielders, get into the habit of "calling" for the ball providing that you intend to make the catch.

Don't hold the ball in the outfield. Always return the ball to the infield as soon as possible to prevent runners from taking an extra base.

Catching a Pop Fly in the Infield

A pop-up or pop fly is a fly ball hit within the infield or one which an infielder attempts to catch.

Follow the same procedures as for catching a fly ball in the outfield.

1. Follow same procedures as for catching fly ball in outfield.

2. Make catch and look to runner(s).

3. Run ball back to infield or throw if runner tries to advance.

Rather than throwing the ball immediately after making the catch, run the ball into the infield, unless, of course, a runner tags up and attempts to advance. However, such a move on his part may be a bluff to draw an erratic throw. Run first then throw if necessary.

Base Play

First Base

Because the **first baseman** receives many throws from infielders and often acts as a cutoff man on throws toward home from the outfield, the ability to range well and catch all types of throws is essential for playing this position.

Whenever a ground ball is hit to another infielder, as a first baseman sprint to first base and straddle the base to face the thrower.

Wait until the throw is made then stretch toward the ball while touching the base with the opposite foot. For a throw to the right-field side of first base, providing you are right-handed, tag the base with your right foot and stretch forward with your left leg to make a backhanded catch. This maneuver affords maximum range; however, some right-handed first basemen may prefer to step off with the right foot to face the ball more directly.

If you throw from the left side, merely step off with your right leg and tag the base with your right foot.

For a throw to the home-plate side of first base, as a right-handed thrower, step toward the throw with the left leg while tagging the base with the right foot.

Should you throw with your left hand, step with your right leg and tag the base with your left foot to make a backhanded catch.

1. Sprint to first base and straddle base to face throw.
2. Wait until throw is made before stretching toward ball.
3. Leave base if throw is very wide, then tag runner or base after catch.

4. Right-handed throwers: To catch throws to right-field side, step out with left leg, tag base with right foot for backhanded catch. Left-handed throwers: For throws to right-field side, step out with right leg and tag base with left foot.

5. Right-handed throwers: For catch to home-plate side, step out with left leg and tag base with right foot. Left-handed throwers: To make catch to home-plate side, step with right leg and tag base with left foot to make backhanded catch.

Catching Low Throws Into the Dirt

Throws into the dirt can be troublesome, even for the veteran player.

A quick pair of hands and good concentration are important factors in developing the ability to dig out low throws. Most importantly, keep your eye on the ball and do not jerk your head away when the ball skids into the dirt.

Throws to Second Base from First Base

After fielding a ground ball, tagging first base or taking a throw, a left-handed first baseman has the advantage of being able to throw to second without first taking a skip step.

A right-handed first baseman should take a short hop on the right foot toward second to get in position for throw to the infielder covering the base.

Whether throwing from the left or right side, the ball should not cross the path of the runner.

After fielding a ground ball and making the subsequent throw, sprint back toward first base then slow your momentum upon nearing the base to take the return throw for a double play if the situation merits.

1. Right-handed first basemen: Take skip step, then throw to second. Left-handed first basemen: Not necessary to take hop step before throw.
2. Do not throw in direct line with runner.
3. After throw, sprint to bag for return throw to complete double play.

Holding a Runner at First Base

Stand with your right foot next to the base and face the pitcher.

As soon as the pitcher delivers the ball toward the plate, sprint to your fielding position and set yourself for a possible play.

1. Stand with right foot next to base.

2. Sprint to fielding position after pitcher delivers ball.

Second Base

A **shortstop** should have the ability to move quickly to the ball, then make a strong, accurate throw after fielding the ball smoothly.

In fielding a ball "deep in the hole" as a shortstop, move in such a way as to surround the ball by keeping your shoulders turned toward first base. Apply all basic techniques in fielding the ball, anchor the right foot and then push off the right foot toward first base. A full turn, overhand throw with maximum wrist snap is necessary for the long carry to first base. Such a play offers the shortstop a most demanding challenge.

It may be impossible to get in front of a ball hit between you and the third baseman, making a backhand stab necessary. After making such a play, be sure to anchor the right foot before attempting to throw.

Without setting up properly, the chances of an inaccurate throw are greatly increased.

A strong arm is a most important requisite for good shortstop play. Usually, the shortstop has the "best arm" in the infield, therefore is called upon as relay man for throws from the deep outfield.

In playing shortstop, practice to develop a strong, accurate throwing arm.

A **second baseman** should be able to throw quickly and accurately without always stepping toward first.

This means that as a second baseman you must throw sidearm or underhand across the body when the situation calls for a quick release. Such may be the case after fielding a slowly hit ground ball or in making the pivot at second base for a double-play attempt.

1. Shortstop play requires good range and a strong, accurate throwing arm.

2. Second base position demands quick hands for handling ball and release to first base.

Covering Second Base on a Steal Attempt

The shortstop and second baseman should agree in advance, either vocally or by signal, who is to cover second base on a steal attempt.

Sprint to the base as soon as the steal is verified. Be in position to shift right or left in case the catcher's throw is off target.

As soon as catch is made, sweep your glove down and into position for the tag.

1. Determine who is to cover second base.

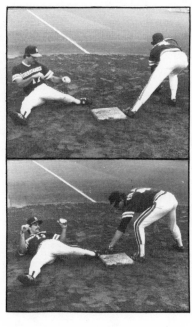

2. As soon as steal is verified, sprint to base. Be in position to shift right or left to make catch.

3. Sweep glove downward quickly to make tag.

Shortstop-Second Baseman Double Play

Both the shortstop and second baseman must learn how to tag second base and then throw quickly to first base.

There are numerous variations of how to tag second base, each depending on where and when the ball is received in relation to the base.

Ideally, the ball should arrive about chest high slightly before reaching the base. The shortstop tags the base with the right foot, whereas the second baseman makes the tag with the left foot. Both players should take another step or so to move clear of the incoming runner while beginning the arm motion for throw to first base.

The pivot man must determine whether to settle for a force out at second or to continue with the double-play attempt. Always make sure of the out at second. Practice often with your counterpart at second base to develop the timing necessary to double-play success.

1. Apply good fielding technique to secure ground ball as pivot man breaks to cover base.

2. Throw to hit pivot man chest high as he nears second base.

3. Second baseman tags base with left foot.

4. Shortstop tags base with right foot then moves clear of runner for throw to first base.

5. Make sure of out at second by keeping eyes on ball and tagging base.

Variations in Tagging the
Base for Double Play

The pivot man at second tags the base according to which side of the base the throw is received.

Second Baseman Receiving the Ball
to Outfield/Third Base Side

Second Baseman Receiving the Ball
to Infield/First Base Side

Shortstop Receiving the Ball to the Infield Side

Shortstop Receiving the Ball to the Outfield Side

Force-Out at Second Base

With two outs in the inning and a runner on first base, it may be more advantageous for a fielder to throw to second base for the third out than to throw to first.

On balls hit to the left side of the infield, the second baseman covers the bag; on balls hit to the right side, the shortstop would cover.

To make the force-out, sprint to the bag and then straddle the base as a first baseman does at first. From this point the mechanics of catching the ball and tagging the base are the same as those for making an out at first.

Third Base

A **third baseman** must have very quick reactions since he often fields the ball an instant after it is hit. The position requires that the third baseman have a reasonably strong arm since throws from third have to be thrown, not merely tossed or lobbed.

As in the case of playing any spot in the infield or outfield, position relative to each batter is important, especially so for a third baseman since he may have less time to react.

As a third baseman, very often after spearing a hard-hit ground ball you will have time to skip step then measure your throw to first. At other times you may be required to field a bunt and throw to first in one motion.

Two points to remember when fielding a bunt or slowly hit ball:

1. Turn shoulders toward first base while fielding ball.
2. When throwing with underhand motion, turn wrist counterclockwise prior to throw for greater accuracy.

Third to Second to First Double Play

One of the most exciting plays in baseball is the third to second to first double play. Timing and accuracy are of the essence since the third baseman most generally has to throw when the pivot man is still running toward second. Also, the ball must be delivered to a spot where the pivot man can handle it quickly then throw to first.

The mechanics are the same as for the "Shortstop-Second Baseman Double Play." However, the greater distance element adds another variable affecting the time available to complete the play and the accuracy for successful execution.

Force-Out at Third Base

Runners on second and first with one or nobody out would present one situation where a third baseman may be required to force the lead runner at third. Merely straddle the bag and react as a first baseman would at first to make the out.

1. Straddle the bag.

2. React right or left as a first baseman would.

Home Plate

Often the **catcher** is referred to as the "quarterback" of the baseball team since he can oversee the entire field from his position behind the plate. He should possess good stamina and leadership ability. Like a first baseman, the catcher must be able to catch balls thrown high, wide or low into the dirt.

Apart from receiving pitches, as a catcher you may be called upon to cover home plate, field bunts or high choppers, back up plays at first base, position players within the infield or outfield and often determine which infielder should catch a pop fly.

Force-Out at Home Plate

A force-out at home should be handled in much the same way that a force-out is at any base. Stand with the base between your feet, a position which allows you to move right or left with equal eaase.

Because home plate is not a raised base as the other bases are, some catchers feel more secure by keeping the left foot on the base while stepping right or left with the right foot. Whereas the range may not be as great as with the straddle method, there isn't the chance of missing the base with the foot.

Regardless of which method you prefer, after making the force-out at home, continue your forward motion to throw to first for the double play.

1. Straddle base in preparation for force-out.

2. Move in direction of ball while tagging base with foot.

Blocking the Plate for Tag-Out

Since home plate is the scoring base, a catcher is called upon to protect the plate in addition to attempting to tag out the runner.

By blocking the plate, the catcher hopes to cause the runner to take a less direct route to the plate, thereby affording more time and a better position to make the tag.

1. Stand in fair territory at a 45-degree angle to each foul line of plate.

2. Crouch in low position.

3. Give runner only one corner of plate to slide toward.

4. Catch ball and move to make tag. Let one motion flow into the other.

Catching the Pop Fly or Foul Ball

Because of a catcher's close proximity to a pop fly in front of the plate or a high foul behind, problems of getting oriented and assessing where the ball will come down present a special challenge.

Turn left for balls hit over your left shoulder and right for balls hit over your right shoulder. As you turn, take off your mask then throw it in the opposite direction to the ball after locating the ball. Locate the ball first then throw the mask.

Balls hit in the home plate area have a tendency to drift back toward the infield. Therefore, be careful not to run too far under the ball. For this reason, playing the ball well in front of you with your back to the infield allows for this infield drift due to the spin on the ball.

Some catchers prefer to catch the ball "breadbasket" style with both hands while others make the catch at chest level much like an outfielder would.

Let one of the infielders catch the ball when possible. The infielder has the advantage of following the ball from the moment it is hit, therefore is able to assess where the ball will come down more easily.

1. Turn in direction of hit while removing mask.

2. Locate ball then throw mask in opposite direction.

3. Play ball in front of you with back to infield, allowing for infield drift.

4. Catch ball with both hands.

The Run-Down Play

The first priority for the defense when it has a runner trapped between bases is to make the out as quickly as possible to prevent other runners from advancing.

When the defense has a base runner in the "hot box," these points should be kept in mind:

1. It should not take more than two throws, and one would be ideal.

2. The defensive player with the ball must run as hard as he can, to make the base runner commit himself.

3. The defensive player should hold the ball high in the air, ready to throw with a wrist-snap motion at any time. Constantly faking the ball is not good technique as it takes too long.

4. The defensive player waiting for the ball should position himself on the throwing side of the player with the ball.

5. When he wants the ball, the defensive player should raise his gloved hand, take one step forward, and yell "now." This enables the player with the ball to start his motion toward the runner before the ball is thrown, thus giving him an opportunity to overtake the runner as the runner retreats.

6. The player with the ball, running as hard as he can, must keep his eyes on his teammate, not the base runner. When he feels he has the runner going back to the base, or when he hears "now" from his teammate, he releases the ball as if he were throwing a dart, with a soft throw high and away from the runner's body.

7. After throwing the ball to a teammate, the player should hustle out of the baseline, not giving the runner an opportunity to bump into him and create an "obstruction" play. Ideally, a third defensive player will take his place in the baseline in case a throw back is necessary. The first defender then follows his throw to the bag and waits there for another throw should one become necessary.

When the run-down play fails to work, it is usually because the first player with the ball did not get the runner to commit. Or secondly, the play fails because the defender with the ball held on to the ball too long while trying to make the tag himself. Finally, when he throws, the ball and runner get to the base at the same time, making it a difficult tag for the defensive player waiting for the ball.

Pitching

Windup and Delivery

Place the forward foot (throwing arm side) in contact with the front edge of the pitcher's plate and the opposite foot directly behind the rubber.

To begin the windup motion shift your weight forward, over the front foot. Bend slightly forward at the waist and swing the throwing arm back naturally. Note that the knees are also bent slightly.

As the throwing arm swings backward, shift your weight back, then as you bring your pitching arm forward again shift your weight forward appropriately.

Turn your hips and shoulders while moving the rear leg up and the throwing arm to the layback position.

Push off the rubber with your pivot leg and stride forward with the lead leg. Throwing arm swings through layback position and then comes forward.

Lead foot lands flat upon the mound, pointing directly at home plate. Stride and landing of the lead foot are most important in setting up the body to open or uncoil properly. Otherwise, a poor opening may mean that the pitch is delivered across the body rather than thrown with the body behind it.

As the lead foot hits the ground, continue to project body weight forward while pivoting the hips and shoulders to face squarely with the plate. At the same time whip your throwing arm through, toward the point of release. The elbow leads the arm motion.

Snap your wrist to release the ball. At release, the body, shoulder, arm, hand and back foot are moving forward. Continue forward motion with a controlled follow-through.

Complete the follow-through in position, ready to field the ball.

1. Wind up by shifting weight forward, back, then forward and swing pitching arm naturally.

47

2. Cock rear leg forward and up while turning hips and shoulders about the pivot leg.

3. Push off pivot leg and stride forward with lead leg. Throwing arm swings through layback then comes forward.

4. Lead foot lands flat upon mound to point directly at plate, thereby allowing body to open properly.

5. As lead foot hits ground, continue to project body weight forward while pivoting hips and shoulders to face squarely with plate. At same time, whip throwing arm through leading with elbow.

6. As arm comes forward, upper arm is approximately parallel with ground and angle between upper arm and forearm is about 90 degrees.

7. Snap wrist to release ball, continue forward motion with controlled follow-through, and complete follow-through in ready position for fielding ball.

8. Ready Position: Feet nearly in line, weight on balls of feet, knees flexed, bent at waist, head up, and eyes fixed on action.

Pitching from the Stretch Position

The stretch position is used with runners on first, second and sometimes with the bases full. From this position, the pitcher can throw to a base or deliver a pitch to the plate.

To assume the stretch position, stand with the pivot foot (foot on throwing side) against the rubber and the opposite foot forward and in line with the plate. Rest weight on pivot leg.

In the stretch move, bring the ball and glove together overhead, then lower both glove and ball (pitching hand) to pause at about belt level. As the stretch is made, the forward foot is brought somewhat closer to the pivot leg. Before throwing to the plate, a pitcher must pause at least one full second.

From this point the mechanics of the kick and delivery correspond to full windup except that kick might be abbreviated and undertaken more quickly with the pushoff from the rubber.

Note: Some youth baseball league rules do not provide for the stretch motion since leading from a base is not allowed.

Check your league rules as the authority on this point.

The pitcher may move his head in any direction. Once a pitcher makes a move to first base, he must throw. Should he not throw, a balk is called and the runner is awarded second base. The pitcher can bluff a throw to either second or third base without penalty providing his foot is off the pitching plate. He must pitch to the batter once his shoulders and body are committed in that direction.

The move to first is merely a quick pivot and oftentimes a ''short arm'' throw. The throw must be accurate; otherwise, the runner may advance to scoring position.

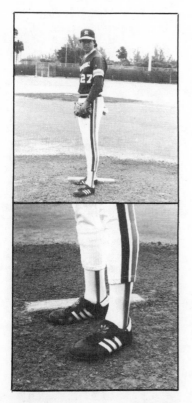

1. Stand with pivot foot against rubber and opposite foot in line with pivot foot and plate. Feet are slightly more than shoulder's-width apart. Rest weight on pivot leg.

2. Bring ball and glove together overhead, then lower glove and pitching hand with ball to about belt level. Pause for at least one second before delivery to plate. Failure to do so results in a balk, and runners advance one base.

3. Look to plate, kick and push off from rubber.

4. Apply good delivery and follow-through technique.

5. Pickoff move to first is a quick pivot and throw.

6. Good follow-through helps accuracy.

7. Timing and coordination with man covering base are most important factors in pickoff move to any base. Practice the pickoff plays often.

The pickoff move to second base is very often a timed play signaled by the catcher to the pitcher and the player covering second, who in turn count silently to themselves at a specified interval so that the throw and the man covering the bag reach the base at the same time.

The Pickoff Move

Left-handed pitchers have an advantage in throwing to first base because they face the base squarely from the stretch position. However, many right-handed pitchers develop a good move to first base even though they have to whirl around to throw.

Run Down of Runner after Pickoff

After a successful pickoff, a runner may choose to break for the next base rather than return to the former base. In such a case, all run-down techniques apply as presented in **the base play section.**

During such a run down, the pitcher has a responsibility to cover a base left uncovered, should the runner evade the run-down attempt.

In a run down between first and second, cover first base; between second and third, cover third; between third and home, cover home.

Types of Pitches

In most cases a pitcher requires a **fast ball, change of pace** and some type of **curve ball** to keep the batter offstride or ''guessing'' as it were.

Youth baseball players are encouraged to concentrate on developing a good fast ball and change of pace while deferring work on a curve ball until the pitching arm and body are more fully matured.

The ball may be delivered with an overhand, three-quarter arm, sidearm or underhand motion. The sidearm and underhand motions put more strain on the arm because it is more difficult to get maximum use of the body behind the pitch. Therefore, pitchers are encouraged to develop a good overhand and three-quarter arm delivery to take advantage of the momentum generated by good body action.

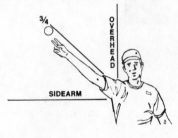

The Fast Ball

The *fast ball* is the mainstay of most pitchers' repertoires. Some fast balls sink, rise on or tail off depending on how the ball is held and how the pitch is released.

The fast ball may be gripped across the seams at the widest point or across the seams at the narrowest point. The thumb usually contacts the seam directly under the fingers.

As you bring your upper arm forward, your upper arm is approximately parallel to the ground and the angle at the elbow is about 90 degrees. The ball leaves your hand slightly forward of the head. At this instant, every ounce of energy (body, arm and wrist-snap) is imparted to the ball.

The wrist-snap is the last crucial moment before delivery. At release, the ball rolls off the fingertips with a clockwise spin.

For the most part, the hand and fingers snap straight downward. Some right-handed pitchers have good success by rotating the hand slightly counterclockwise.

Most importantly, practice to deliver the ball consistently each time and lean to your fast ball for strikes.

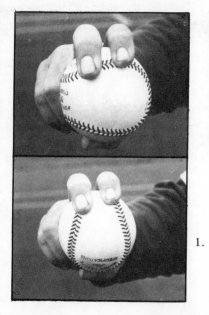

1. Grip fast ball across seams at widest point or at narrowest point. Thumb contacts seam directly underneath fingers.

2. Coordinate forward thrust of body, whiplike motion of arm and snapping-action of wrists to achieve optimum ball velocity.

3. Throw fast ball the same way each time and practice for control.

The Change of Pace

The *change-of-pace* is pitched with a delivery to look like a fast ball, yet the ball travels much more slowly.

Some pitchers grip the ball loosely well in back of the hand and release it with little pressure by the fingers. After releasing the ball, the pitching hand comes straight down quickly to give the appearance of delivering the ball with speed.

Other pitchers retain the normal fast ball grip and achieve the change-of-pace through finger action at the time of release. The fingers are relaxed at the point of release, taking some of the speed off the ball.

In both methods, it may be helpful to drag the pivot foot after releasing from the pitching rubber, thereby taking some of the body's motion from the ball.

Such a pitch is useful in keeping hitters offstride and setting up batters for the fast ball.

1. Grip same as for fast ball or "palm ball."

2. Hold ball in back of hand with little pressure by fingers; or, use normal fast ball grip. Release fingers at point of release to impact change-of-pace action. Deliver ball to look like fast ball. Drag pivot foot, to de-emphasize body's power transferred to ball.

The Curve Ball

A *curve ball* is a ball thrown in such a way as to break and drop when nearing the plate.

To throw a curve, you follow the same basic techniques as for throwing the fast ball except that the grip, hand and wrist action are different at delivery.

The grip resembles the fast ball grip only that you exert more pressure with the second finger and thumb than with the index finger.

58

As you deliver the ball, twist the hand forward and clockwise, a motion similar to releasing a "yo-yo." This motion is coupled with a pronounced snapping action of the wrist.

The ball rolls off the outside of the index finger thus developing the spin necessary to cause the ball to break.

1. Hold ball in similar fashion to fast ball, but exert more pressure with the second finger than with the first.

2. Rotate hand forward and clockwise coupled with pronounced wrist snap. Motion similar to snapping fingers and releasing "Yo-Yo."

3. To increase effectiveness, learn to throw curve with different speeds.

The Slider

Usually a *slider* is thrown with good speed to break quickly but not as much as a curve.

The grip is essentially that of a fast ball, only the ball is held more to the side. Likewise, the ball should be delivered to look like a fast ball only to break quickly at the last moment.

The arm motion is similar to passing a football. The wrist rotates quickly as the ball is released to slide off the index finger.

1. Assume fast ball grip, but hold ball more to side.

2. Arm motion similar to that for making football pass. Wrist rotates quickly in clockwise direction to slide ball off index finger.

Knuckle Balls, Screw Balls, Fork Balls, Etc.

Some pitchers are able to develop a specialty pitch which further complements their repertoire of a **fast ball, change of pace and curve.** Other pitchers develop such pitches after one of the more basic pitches such as the fast ball becomes less effective.

Work to master control of the basic pitches before attempting to add any of the more specialized pitches to your assortment. Professional pitchers may work several seasons on developing such a pitch before throwing it in a game.

A good **knuckle ball** is equally effective against right- or left-handed batters since it breaks rather unpredictably. The pitch is gripped with the thumb underneath and the fingernails of the first two fingers or the first knuckles of the first two fingers on top. Some pitchers are careful to grip the knuckle ball so that no part of the hand touches the seams.

The ball is thrown with the wrist held more stiffly so that it appears to "float" toward the plate because of the little or no spin imparted to the ball and may break several times before reaching the catcher. Because of the nature of the pitch, catchers sometimes have difficulty handling the ball.

A **screw ball** breaks in a direction opposite to a curve. Therefore, such a pitch thrown from the left side is particularly effective against a right-handed batter, and when thrown from the right side effective against a left-handed batter.

The pitch is gripped much like a curve ball only that more pressure is exerted by the index finger rather than the second finger. The left-handed pitcher rotates the wrist in a clockwise direction to throw the pitch, whereas the right-handed pitcher turns the wrist in a counterclockwise direction. Some pitchers are actually able to snap their wrists inward, adding to the effectiveness of the pitch.

A **fork ball** has an action similar in many cases to that of the knuckle ball. The ball is gripped between the first two fingers rather than with these two fingers on top. The ball may be thrown to slide off the second finger or pushed out between the fingers with the thumb causing very little spin.

Tips for Pitchers

Run to condition your legs. Leg strength and endurance are vital to pitching. Often the legs will tire before the arm if the legs are out of shape.

Maximize the use of body motion and momentum to throw each pitch. Don't allow your arm to do all the work. Push off from the rubber and let good body action lend zip to your pitches.

Keep the ball hidden from the batter as long as possible before release. Hold the ball in your glove until the start of the body turn when the ball is withdrawn and thrown with full arm and body action. The glove should lead the throw, thereby further hiding the ball from the batter.

Gain confidence in your ability to throw the ball where you want it to go. Pick out a target — catcher's glove, knee, belt or whatever — and then keep your eyes on that target throughout the pitch. Move your head directly toward the plate so that the release of the ball occurs as far out in front of the pitcher's plate as possible.

Maintain a positive mental attitude while pitching. Don't let errors by teammates or the game situation "blow your mind." Concentrate only on throwing strikes and getting batters out.

Catching a Pitched Ball

Because the pitched ball has great velocity, a catcher has time only to shift one step left or right for pitches away from the plate. Therefore, a catcher must assume a position prior to the pitch which allows him to make this shift quickly.

The Ready Position

Begin in a squat position with feet comfortably spaced apart, knees turned out and left arm resting on thigh. The gloved hand extends beyond the left knee while the throwing hand gives the signals between the legs near the crotch.

After the signal is flashed for the pitch, rise up slightly from the squat position and spread your feet further apart. The right foot is slightly behind the left foot.

The throwing hand should be relaxed with the fingers closed loosely around the thumb. Don't clench your fist.

1. Assume squat position with feet comfortably spaced apart, knees turned out and left arm resting on thigh.

2. Glove hand extends beyond left knee while throwing hand gives signal between legs near crotch.

3. After giving signal, rise up slightly and spread further apart. Right foot is slightly behind left foot.

4. Throwing hand is relaxed with fingers loosely closed around thumb.

Receiving the Pitch

The catcher's position should be as close as possible to the batter without interfering with him. From this position, the glove affords a better target to the pitcher. Also the catcher can handle low pitches and foul tips more easily.

Don't change the position of your hands until after the pitcher has started his delivery. If the pitch is below the waist, your gloved hand should be extended with the palm toward the pitcher and fingers pointing down. For a pitch above the waist, the fingers are pointed upward.

It is most important to receive the ball in the middle portion of the body. To catch the ball simply roll the right hand around the face of the glove to trap the ball in the pocket. Hands and arms "give" toward the body to cushion the impact. Fingers automatically encircle the ball.

5. Assume a position close to batter, but not to close as to interfere with swing.
6. Provide good target for pitcher throughout windup and delivery.
7. Catch balls below waist with palm of glove facing toward pitcher and fingers pointing down.

8. For balls above waist, point fingers upward. As far as possible, catch balls in middle of body.
9. Secure ball in glove with bare hand. Hands and arms give toward body to cushion impact.

The Throw

The game situation pretty much dictates how cautious a catcher has to be behind the plate and what type of throw he should make back to the pitcher or to one of the bases.

With runners on base, turn the hips and shoulders, drawing the ball and glove to the right side after the catch. This body turn will allow use of the entire body, should a throw to one of the bases be necessary. Use a step and full arm throw to a base. A quick but accurate throw is the primary desire.

10. After catch, turn hips and shoulders to draw ball and glove to right side.

11. For power and accuracy, step and use full arm throw to base.

Snap Throw

Some catchers develop a good snap throw which is the quickest means of getting rid of the ball, often to catch a baserunner off the base. This throw utilizes an abbreviated layback with maximum arm and wrist-snap action.

Catching Pitches Away from the Plate

From the basic catching position, merely shift by taking a step in the direction of the ball while holding the opposite foot stationary.

Of course for pitches very wide, more drastic action must be taken and most often very quickly. Sometimes, you may only have time to knock the ball down.

Blocking Pitches into the Dirt

With runners on base, the catcher must either catch the ball or at least keep the ball in front of him. Many catchers become particularly proficient in blocking low pitching to prevent runners from advancing.

Basically it's a matter of keeping your head down to watch the ball, getting your body in front of the ball (usually by dropping to your knees) and then hanging in there.

Tips for Catchers

Learn opposing batters' strengths and weaknesses. To call pitches effectively, you should have some idea of what pitches cause a particular batter problems or in what position in relation to the plate a pitch would be most effective.

Keep signals simple. Signals should be seen only by pitcher, second baseman and shortstop.

Keep on top of the game. As a catcher, you are the key defensive strategist on the field. Your hustle and leadership inspire teammates to play harder.

Develop good rapport with your pitchers. Call time and go out to talk with your pitcher. Calm him down, buoy him up or merely check with him about a game situation.

Hitting

A .300 hitter makes 70 outs in each 100 at-bats. Over half of those outs come on pitches outside the strike zone. Thus, it is very important that each player knows his own strike zone.

Bat control should be the goal of every hitter. Such control is achieved by observing fundamental elements of good hitting — bat selection, the grip, the stance and the swing.

If the hitter gets the bat to the right spot at the right time, it doesn't matter whether it's a fast ball, breaking ball, or change-up, he will make good contact.

Bat Selection

Selecting a proper bat is important in helping to achieve better control, hence more success, translated to mean more base hits. Use of a lighter bat allows a player to wait longer in choosing a pitch to hit.

The Grip

Hold the bat in the fingers, not in the back of the hands. Knuckles of both hands should be lined up evenly. Think of gripping the bat as you would a baseball, for the bat should be "thrown" at the ball. Many hitters will move their hands up from the end of the bat to achieve better balance and control. This is called "choking up."

1. Hold bat in fingers, knuckles aligned.
2. Throw bat at ball.
3. Choke up on bat for better balance and control.

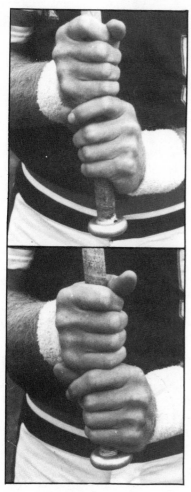

CHOKE GRIP

POWER GRIP

Stance

Stand in a spot that allows a full, comfortable extension of your arms when you swing. Take time to get set up properly and comfortably. A balanced, workable stance enables the batter to shift from a firm, rigid, backside to a firm, rigid frontside. It also insures against muscles locking in tense positions.

Feet should be spread shoulder width apart. The upper body should be bent or crouched slightly from the waist with knees flexed and relaxed. Hands and bat are held over the rear foot. A good reference is to be sure the bat is on position to launch is to touch the bat to the rear shoulder, then raise it to the correct position. This will start you as close as possible to the launching position, giving you quickness, more time to react and making you more consistent.

A closed stance is recommended for all batters. This allows the batter to be quicker with his hands on inside pitches and swing with more power than with an open stance.

PARALLEL

CLOSED

OPEN

1. Feet spread shoulder width.
2. Upper body crouches, knees flexed.
3. Touch bat to rear shoulder, raise to correct position.
4. Extend arms fully on swing.

Swing

Swing aggressively if you swing at all. In striding toward the plate, keep front foot in closed position. The bat must be in the throwing position at the moment the front foot touches down. On inside pitches, think of hitting the ball between second base and the right field line. At the moment of contact, the bat should be straight out in front of you, arms fully extended, head tipped down slightly and behind the point of contact of bat with ball, and eyes on the ball. Be sure to swing through. On balls not swung at, watch the ball into the catcher's glove.

1. Swing aggressively.

2. Tilt head down, eyes on ball.

3. Swing through ball.

Rhythm and Movement

Good rhythm and movement are essential to becoming a good hitter. A batter must move back before he can move forward.

As the pitcher delivers the ball, shift your weight back to the rear foot with a slight inward turn. This will cock your shoulders and hips, preventing you from losing power by opening your shoulders and hips too soon your swing. Your weight should be almost entirely on your rear foot.

As the pitch approaches the plate, your forward foot should simultaneously glide toward home plate as you push off from the inside of your back foot to being uncoiling movement, subsequently launching the bat.

Find a correct, comfortable position for your head. The easiest way to do this is to have your head in a position that enables you to follow the pitch with both eyes.

Remember, as you swing, your head should tilt down with eyes open, watching the ball as long as possible. If the pitch is a ball, follow it into the catcher's glove.

1. Shift weight back as pitcher delivers.
2. As pitch nears plate, glide forward foot toward plate and push off from inside of rear foot.
3. Follow the pitch with both eyes.

Bunting

A bunter's stance should be such as to allow coverage of the entire plate with the bat.

To bunt the ball in a sacrifice situation, assume the normal batting ready position as the pitcher begins the windup.

When the pitcher takes the ball out of his glove, pivot on the front foot to face the pitcher squarely by bringing the back foot up parallel with the front. Some bunters prefer to step back slightly with the front foot while turning and bringing the back foot up rather than pivoting with the front foot in place.

As you turn to face the pitcher, slide your top hand up the bat handle to a spot close to the trademark. Four fingers support the bat from underneath with the thumb on top.

The forearm of the forward arm is about parallel with the ground and forms nearly a 90-degree angle with the upper arm at the elbow. Body is crouched forward slightly, head is up, arms relaxed and bat is parallel with the ground.

1. Assume normal batting stance. As pitcher takes ball out of glove to throw, square around to face him.

2. As you pivot to face pitcher, slide top hand up bat handle to spot near trademark.

3. Forearm of forward arm about parallel with ground, forming 90-degree angle with upper arm at elbow.

4. Sacrifice bunting position: Body crouched forward slightly, weight forward, arms relaxed and bent at elbows, bat parallel with ground, head up, and eyes on ball.

Contacting the Ball

As the ball approaches, try to keep the bat as level as possible. Get the bat in front of the ball by raising or lowering your body from the knees and waist. Move your arms as little as possible.

Let the ball hit the bat. Upon contact the bat recoils into the ''V'' formed by the thumb and forefinger of the upper hand. This action deadens the impact and prevents the ball from bouncing too far.

A newer technique theory suggests that you hold the bat in a more vertical position with the barrel of the bat pointing slightly downward to insure a ground ball. While this technique has yet to be proven fully, it does present some interesting possibilities.

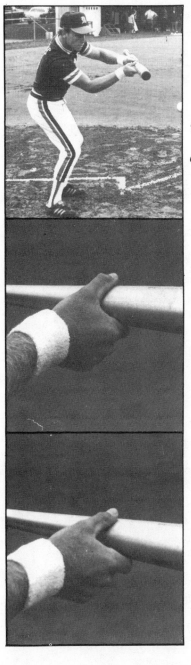

5. Keep bat as level as possible as ball approaches.
6. Get bat in front of ball by raising or lowering body from knees and waist. Move arms as little as possible.

7. Upon contact, bat recoils to "V" space formed by fingers and thumb to deaden impact.

Bunting for a Base Hit

Most all bunting techniques apply, except that the batter should wait until the last moment before committing himself to the bunt.

When bunting for a hit, pick a pitch which will afford you the fastest start to first base. Then simply step toward the pitch with your forward foot and bring your bat into bunting position. Hold the bat firmly with your lower hand and rather loosely with the top hand to apply all bunting fundamentals.

Bunting Tips

Unless "suicide squeeze play" is on, bunt only strikes. If the suicide squeeze is on, the ball must be bunted.

Action of the back hand should complement that of the forward hand. Hold firm with the bottom hand and more loosely with the top hand to provide the "softening" action necessary for a successful bunt.

All players should learn to bunt properly. Pitchers should practice bunting often since they frequently are called upon to execute the sacrifice bunt.

Because the left-handed hitter is a step or two closer to first base, the drag bunt may be particularly advantageous. Both right- and left-handed hitters with good speed can bunt for a base hit with good success, thereby getting on base to help the team and adding percentage points to their batting average. Even slower runners can surprise the defense with a well-placed bunt. Make sure bat is out in front of plate. This helps to keep ball in fair territory.

Things to Remember

Unless the "count" dictates otherwise, plan to swing on every pitch until your mind tells you it's a ball.

A short, compact, aggressive swing will make you a better hitter.

Have good rhythm and weight shift. Be aggressive and keep your eyes on the ball. Try to watch the ball hit the bat.

Do not lunge at the ball as it causes the upper body to move too far forward too fast. The lunge is not a rhythmic move.

Keeping the forward foot in a closed position, stride toward the plate, not toward the pitcher. This prevents hips and shoulders from opening too soon, which causes a loss of power, and enables you to keep your eyes on the ball better and gives you a better chance to hit the outside pitch. If hips and shoulders open too soon, the upper body is pulled out of position and the head turns, bringing your eyes off the ball.

Unless you are trying to hit a sacrifice fly, avoid the upper cut swing which collapses the rear leg, forces front shoulder up and hampers weight shift, causing hips to open too soon.

Relax at the plate. If you are tense, your body can not move smoothly because your muscles are rigid, making it impossible to have a smooth-flowing, head-down swing.

Wait on the ball. Most unsuccessful batters have a quick bat. They react too soon, stepping and swinging at the same time. To hit well, the step and swing must be two distinctive movements.

Know your strike zone, be patient and only swing at strikes. The poor hitter or hitter in a slump will lose patience, swing at bad balls and become tense, creating a bad swing.

A level or slightly downward swing is better than swinging upward. Hitting ground balls is better than hitting fly balls. The more the defense has to handle the ball, the more chances it has to make mistakes.

Use the entire field to hit in.

Baserunning

The all-out sprint between the batter's box and first base starts immediately after the ball is hit. No time should be lost in watching the ball. Even the time it takes to glance in the direction of the ball may mean the difference between reaching the base safely and being out.

Running to First Base

The swing of a right-handed hitter carries him away from first base; therefore it is best to start by pushing off with the left foot and throwing the body in the direction of first base.

The first step is with the right foot and from there it is merely a matter of beating the throw to the bag.

The momentum from a left-handed hitter's swing carries him toward first base. Pushing off on the ball of the right foot and leaning the body in the direction of first base takes advantage of this momentum.

If it appears that it will be a close play at the bag, run just to the right of the foul line and tag the base in full stride. To insure that you do not slow up when nearing the base, select a spot some 10 strides beyond the bag and run toward it.

Your first-base coach will tell you if there is a chance for an extra base. If such is the case, run a tight circle pattern by moving out of the base line then arc back to tag the inside corner of the base in full stride. Keep on going if you think that you can reach second safely. If not, slow your run and return to first base quickly.

Right

1. Right-handed hitters push off with left foot toward first, whereas left-handed hitters push off from right foot.

Left

2. Run to a spot some 10 strides beyond bag to insure tagging base in full stride.

3. With possibility of going to second, run tight circle pattern and tag inside corner of base in full stride.

4. If going to second base is not practical, slow run and return quickly to first.

5. Running bases is merely a continuation of flat arc started at first base.

Taking the Leadoff

The type of lead which you choose to take depends on such factors as the game situation (Does it call for a steal or hit-and-run play?), the ability of the pitcher to make a move to first base, your speed and quickness and your general baserunning ability.

The *one-way lead* is one in which you commit your weight in the direction which you intend to run. Such a lead permits you to get a good start toward the next base. Obviously with your weight toward second, your return to first is somewhat more difficult, should the pitcher throw over there.

One suggestion is to take a slightly shorter lead so as not to draw the throw.

For a *two-way lead,* you assume a more balanced position allowing you to break for the next base or return to the former base with equal ease.

A *walking lead* is especially effective, against a pitcher who is careless about checking a runner at first. Also, this leadoff should be used when leading off of third base. Simply walk slowly toward the next base and then make your break when you determine the pitcher is going to the plate with the ball.

Regardless of the type of lead which you employ, once you have decided to run for the next base, run! Don't hesitate.

1. When holding a base, stand with your left foot touching inside edge of bag. Keep foot on base until pitcher begins wind-up or stretch motion.

2. Take leadoff in direct line with base. Watch pitcher closely.

3. Be prepared to return to base. Note: when leading off of third, walk to the inside (foul side) of foul line to avoid getting hit with batted ball. If ball isn't hit, pivot into baseline for return to third, making catcher's throw more difficult.

4. Turn body in direction of run, push off with right foot and take first step with left foot.

5. Once committing yourself to run for next base, run — don't hesitate.

Sliding into a Base

A *slide into a base* is undertaken to avoid being tagged out.

Approach the bag with your body erect and your eyes on the base. Take off for the slide on whichever foot is most natural to you.

Immediately after taking off, bend the takeoff leg underneath to buf-`er the shock of landing on the ground, then raise the opposite leg well ,ff the ground and extend it toward the base. Be sure the bent leg is turned sideways to avoid catching the spikes in the ground.

The brunt of the slide is absorbed on the lower part of the hip and back of the upper thigh. To avoid injury, do not slide on the foreleg portion of the leg. Contact the nearest corner or side of the bag with the extended foot. Once reaching the bag, let the momentum of the slide help you regain your feet to advance another base if possible. This type of slide, called *the straight-in slide, the pop-up slide* or *bent-leg slide,* is most basic.

In some cases on a close play at the base, you may prefer to remain in a prone position rather than continuing through to the standing position. However, be careful not to stop so quickly as to twist your ankle or jam your leg.

1. Approach bag with body erect and eyes on base. Take off on whichever foot you prefer.

94

2. After takeoff, bend takeoff leg underneath and extend opposite leg toward base. Bent leg helps to cushion fall to ground. Slide on lower hip and back of upper thigh.

3. Contact nearest side of base.
4. Let momentum carry you forward to regain your feet.

Hook Slide

The *hook slide* is one variation of the more basic straight-in slide whereby a runner hopes to present a more elusive target for a tag.

The approach to the bag is basically the same as for the straight-in slide, except that both feet are turned sideways and directed toward the bag. Rather than sliding in a direct line to the base, slide either to the right or left of the base.

In sliding to the left, hook the corner of the bag with your right foot; in sliding to the right, hook the corner with your left foot.

When the ball arrives at base first, some alert runners will slide past the base then reach back with their hand to avoid the tag. Obviously, this sliding method is merely a last resort tactic to avoid a tag.

One further note: the *head-first slide* generally has proven to be dangerous, therefore is to be discouraged.

1. Both feet are turned sideways and directed toward the base.

2. Hook corner of base with foot nearest base.

3. Note scissorlike action of legs as slide is completed.

Rules Simplified

Dimensions

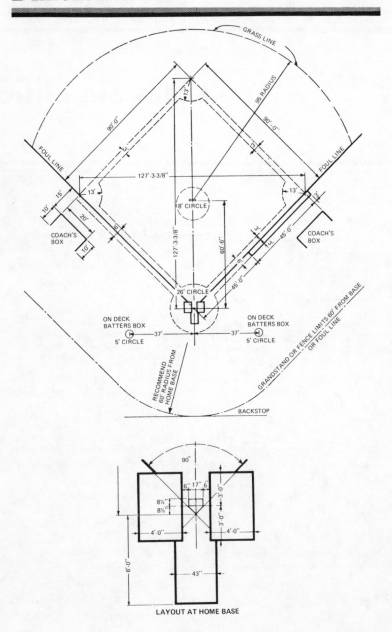

LAYOUT AT HOME BASE

Today's baseball is a very different ball than the rubber ball used years ago. Now, the ball is constructed with a cork or rubber center, a tight wool winding and a horsehid cover.

Each player is required to wear a mitt (glove), the type of which is prescribed by rules of the game relative to the position played. For instance, a player cannot wear a first baseman's glove ("trapper model") when playing in the outfield.

Bats are scientifically designed and standardized in various sizes to accommodate the physical attributes and personal preferences of all ball players.

The baseball diamond is 90 feet on each side (90' between bases). Lines extend straight out from home plate beyond first and third base to separate fair from foul territory.

The batter's box on either side of home plate is four feet by six feet. Home plate itself is 17 inches wide and 17 inches from the front to the back corner.

The pitcher and catcher as a pair are known as the battery. The distance from the front of the pitcher's plate to the back corner of home plate is 60 feet, six inches.

The first baseman, the second baseman, the shortstop and the third baseman are known as infielders. Completing the nine-man team and known as the outfields are the right fielder, the center fielder and the left fielder.

A game is divided into nine innings. Each team is allowed one turn at bat per inning. With the third out, a team's turn at bat ends. That team then takes the field and the opposing team bats. Rules provide that a game be as many as nine innings long. Specific league rules may provide that a game be shorter.

The team with the greatest number of runs at the end of nine innings is the winner. A run is scored when a runner touches home plate preceded by tagging first, second and third bases. Extra innings are played to determine the winner of a game tied after the end of regulation play. An official game may be recorded after five innings (after 4½ innings if the home team is leading) should rain or inclement weather cause play to be suspended.

For official rules, consult the following sources:

All American Amateur Baseball Assn.
R.D. 5, Box 316A
Johnstown, Pennsylvania 15905

American Amateur Baseball Congress
Stan Musial, Connie Mack
Mickey Mantle and Sandy Koufax Divisions
P.O. Box 5332
Akron, Ohio 44313

American Legion
Box 1055
Indianapolis, Indiana 46206

Babe Ruth Baseball
524½ Hamilton Avenue
Trenton, New Jersey 08609

Boys Baseball, Inc.
P.O. Box 225
Washington, Pennsylvania 15301

George Khoury Baseball
3222 Park Avenue
St. Louis, Missouri 63104

Little League Baseball, Inc.
P.O. Box 1127
Williamsport, Pennsylvania 17701

National Baseball Congress
Box 1420
Wichita, Kansas 62201

National Hot Stove Baseball League, Inc.
210 East Main Street
Alliance, Ohio 44601

The Sporting News
1212 N. Lindberg Blvd.
St. Louis, Missouri 63166

Learn to Keep Score

Keeping a scorecard adds interest to watching a baseball game, whether at a high school field or a major league stadium. It keeps the scorer actively involved in the game's progress and can also make a nice souvenir.

The usual scoring system follows the player around the diamond, starting at home plate on the lower part of the infield design and moving in a counter clockwise direction to first, second and third base, then back to home.

Every way of getting on base, except fielder's choice, is noted down the right side of the box. When a batter reaches base, draw a line to that base and indicate on the right border how he reached. A completed line around the diamond represents a run. An incompleted diamond shows that the runner was left on base when the inning ended.

POSITION NUMBERS OF PLAYERS

1	Pitcher	4	Second Baseman	7	Left Fielder
2	Catcher	5	Third Baseman	8	Center Fielder
3	First Baseman	6	Shortstop	9	Right Fielder

ACTION DURING PLAY

KS	Strikeout swinging	PB	Passed Ball	AB	Times at bat
KC	Strikeout called	WP	Wild Pitch	R	Runs
E	Error	DP	Double play	H	Hits
B	Balk	TP	Triple Play	RBI	Runs batted in
O	Out	SB	Stolen Base		
FO	Force Out	OS	Outstealing		
SH	Sacrifice hit	FC	Fielder's choice		
SF	Sacrifice fly	DH	Designated hitter		

Here is a sample scorecard from three innings played by the University of Miami.

First Inning: Wrona (SS) led off with a home run. Shields (CF) walked, stole second base. Seoane (2B) ground out, shortstop to first base. Lane (3B) doubled to center, scoring Shields. Lusby (1B) grounded out, second to first, a fielder's choice, Lane going to third. Velasquez (LF) flied out to right. 2 runs, 2 hits.

University of Miami Scorecard ____ vs. _ .

	PLAYERS	POS	1	2	3	4
17	Bill Wrona	6	◆ 6	K		
	sub. Sacco	PR 8				
5	Doug Shields	8	◆ SB 5	1-3		
	Sub.					
14	Mitch Seoane	4	6-3		◆ 3	
	Sub.					
7	Phil Lane	5	◇		◆ DH	
	Sub.					
12	Steve Lusby	3	4-3 FC		◆ DH	
	Sub.					
33	Javier Valasquez	7	F-9		Kc	
	Sub.					
4	Don Rowland	DH		◆ SB 9	◇	
	Sub.					
35	Calvin James	9		◇	5-4	
	Sub.					
9	Bob Walker	2		F-9	D.P. 5-4-3	2
	Sub. Artiles	PH 8				
	Sub.					

Scoremaster P.O. BOX 46036, HOLLYWOOD, CALIF 90046

Second Inning: Rowland (DH) walked, stole second base. James (RF) singled to left, scoring Rowland. Walker flied out to right. Wrona struck out. Shields grounded out, pitcher to first. 1 run, 1 hit.

Third Inning: Seoane doubled to right-center. Lane walked. Lusby singled to center, scoring Seoane. Velasquez called out on strikes. Rowland doubled to left, scoring Lane and Lusby. James walked. Walker hit into 5-4-3 double play. Third base to second base, forcing James, to first base. 3 runs, 3 hits.

Basic Strategy
and Tactics

Offense

Hit to Opposite Field

"Go with the pitch" means that the hitter hits a ball thrown on the outside part of the plate to the opposite field and a left-handed hitter would hit the ball to the right field and a left-handed hitter would hit to left field.

Hit and Run

The *hit and run plays* simply means that a runner or runners will break (or run) toward the next base as the pitcher throws to the hitter. The batter has the obligation to hit the ball sharply on the ground if possible, hopefully through the infield position to cover the base for the steal. It is wise that the hitter be ahead of the pitcher 2-0, or better still, 3-1 to insure that the pitcher throws a strike. Runners should be careful not to get picked off base when the hit and run is on.

Sacrifice Bunt

"Sacrifice bunt" is so called because the hitter sacrifices his chance to hit so as to advance a runner or runners to another base. The bunter squares around or turns his body to face the pitcher when the pitcher takes the ball out of his glove to throw.

Delayed Steal

A *delayed steal* occurs when a baserunner waits or delays until the catcher starts to throw the ball back to the pitcher, then breaks for the next base.

Also, with runners on first and third it means that the runner on first breaks for second to draw the catcher's throw. As the catcher throws, the runner on third breaks for the plate. However, the runner on third must be careful that an infielder does not cut the ball off and return it quickly to the catcher.

Squeeze Plays

There are two types of *squeeze plays:* the safety squeeze and the suicide squeeze. A runner on third breaks for home only at the end of his walking lead off third when the hitter bunts the ball on the ground. This is called a safety squeeze. In the suicide squeeze the runner on third breaks toward home at the moment the pitcher releases the pitch. The batter waits until the pitcher releases the ball before he gives himself up to bunt the ball on the ground. Occasionally there will be runners on second and third when the squeeze is used. The runner on second will try to score while the fielder is trying to throw out the bunter. This play is called the double squeeze.

Sacrifice Fly

A *sacrifice fly* occurs when a runner on third can tag up and score after the ball is caught. The hitter is not credited with a time at bat under such a situation and is credited with a run batted in.

Defense

Relief Pitching Stragegy

Often a left-handed pitcher will be brought in to pitch to a left-handed hitter. This stratagem is used because left-handed hitters usually have more difficulty hitting the curve ball breaking away from them; or it is used to force the offense to use a hitter who bats right. However, this theory doesn't always work. Much depends on the ability and "stuff" a pitcher has rather than whether he is left-or right-handed.

Pitchout

If the catcher anticipates a stolen base attempt, he should signal the pitcher to throw the ball high and outside the strike zone so that he can best throw to second.

Positioning the Team Defensively

Depending upon whether a batter usually hits to left field, right field or straightaway, members of the team on defense should make positioning adjustments to compensate accordingly.

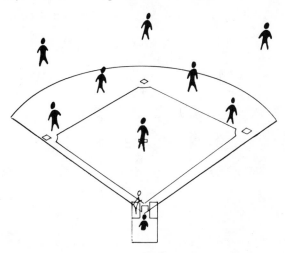

Alignment of a team on defense for a batter who hits straightaway.

Overshift for Pull Hitters

An overshifted infield defense occurs whenever the infielders move three or four steps from their normal defensive positions such as toward their right (for a right-handed hitter) because the hitter normally "pulls" the ball toward left field.

In cases where a batter is an extremely strong and consistent pull hitter, a manager may choose to position three infielders on one side of the infield leaving only one fielder on the other side.

Alignment to compensate for a batter who usually hits to left field.

Defensive positioning for a batter who usually hits to right field.

Fielders usually play deeper for power hitters and more shallow for weaker hitters. Other adjustments may be necessary as the game situation merits.

Defensive Alignment Late in a Close Game

Late in a close game the first and third basemen should play closer to the foul lines, guarding them to prevent possible extra base hits down the lines. Outfielders should play deeper and the right and left fielders should move toward center (or "bunch").

Defensive Alignment of Infield with Two Out and Runners on First and Second

All the infielders should play deeper than normal to prevent a ground ball from getting through. This permits a force out at any base.

Play at the Plate

With a runner on third and less than two out, the strategy may call for the infielder to play in more closely to the batter for an attempt to throw out the runner at home on a ground ball hit within the infield.

Backing Up the Play in the Infield

Aside from fielding and base coverage responsibilities, each infielder must back up teammates on batted and thrown balls. Back-up positions are determined by where the play is developing.

The pitcher backs up the third baseman on throws to third
and backs up the catcher on throws to home plate.

The pitcher covers home when the catcher is drawn away
from the plate

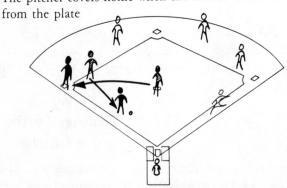

When the third baseman is pulled away from the base as
in the case of fielding a bunt, the pitcher covers third base.

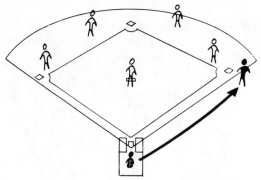

The catcher backs up the first baseman on throws to first base.

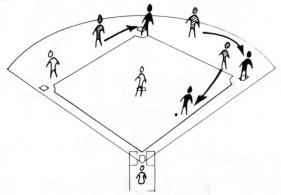

The second baseman covers first base when the first baseman is pulled out of position to field a bunt.

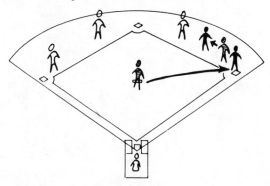

When the first baseman moves to his right to field a ground ball, the pitcher covers first base. Note that the first baseman may recover in time to tag the base himself. However, on

111

ground balls hit to the first baseman's right, it is always a good practice for the pitcher to break toward first base in case his coverage is necessary.

Either the shortstop or the second baseman may cover second base. When the second baseman covers first base, the shortstop is responsible for second base.

The shortstop backs up the second baseman when the second basemen is covering the base. Conversely, when the shortstop covers the base, the second baseman backs up the play.

Backing Up the Play
in the Outfield

Aside from fielding the ball, outfielders also are responsible for backing up infielders on hit or thrown balls as well as for backing up the play of fellow outfielders.

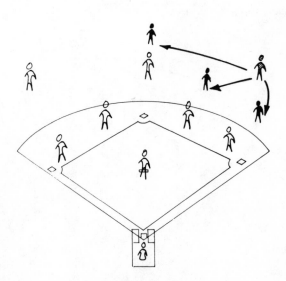

The right fielder backs up the first baseman, second baseman or the center fielder depending upon where the play develops.

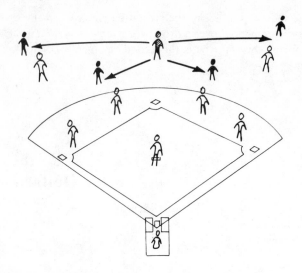

The center fielder is responsible for backing up the right fielder, the left fielder, the second baseman and the shortstop.

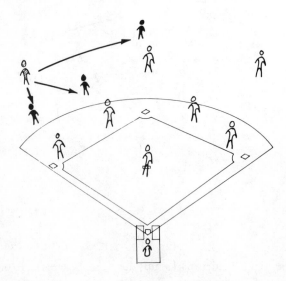

The left fielder backs up the center fielder, the third baseman and the shortstop.

Basic Drills

Batting Cage Drills

Half-Bat Drills

Develops hand quickness, and hand, wrist and forearm strength. Player uses half-bat, the top half of a sawed off wooden bat, because it is too hard to swing a full bat with one hand. The player kneels on his rear knee with his front knee off the ground. Another player tosses balls underhand to the batter from a slightly forward angle. The batter places the half-bat in his left hand and takes approximately 25 swings, then switches the half-bat to his right hand and takes about 25 more swings.

Standing Hit-Downs

Batter stands approximately eight feet from a chain link fence or screen with a regular baseball bat. Another player is angled near the fence and tosses balls underhand to the batter, aiming at his hip. The batter should take about 50 of these swings. This drill develops bat quickness and helps the batter keep his weight back while also working on different pitching areas.

Soft-Toss Drill

Similar to regular batting practice in a cage except the pitcher is sitting in a chair behind a protective screen and is approximately 20 feet in front of the batter. This drill helps the batter's quickness and improves strike zone recognition. Also, the drill does not take a lot of effort by the pitcher.

Batting Practice Drills

Off-Center Screen Drill

The screen is moved to the left or to the right of the pitcher's mound. If the screen is to the left, or first base side, assistance can be given to right-handed batters who need work on hitting to the opposite field and left-handed batter who need work on pulling the ball. When the screen is on the third base side of the pitcher's mound, there is help for right-handed batters who need to work on pulling the ball and left-handed batters who need work on hitting the ball to the opposite field.

The idea in this drill is that by changing the angle of the pitch, hitters trying to pull are forced to throw the bat out in front of the plate in order to hit the ball. For the batter trying to go to the opposite field, he must try to hit the ball behind the plate, since it is almost impossible to pull the ball from the angle it is pitched.

Specializing Situation Hitting

At the end of each round of batting practice, we set up situations and try to hit the ball accordingly. We usually go for 3 hit-and-runs, 3 hit to the opposite field, 3 getting player in from third base with less than two outs, and 3 regular. We feel this drill should improve the ability of our players to perform better in a game, when they face similar situations.

Mini-Drills for Infielders

These drills provide infielders with numerous opportunities to improve fielding fundamentals.

Position two players at each spot in the infield. Place a protective screen 30 feet up the line from first base toward second base and place first baseman on second base side of screen to take throws from second base.

Fungos are hit from the third base side and first base side of home plate. Each fungo hitter should have one shagger.

With first baseman on second base side of screen, work on 5-4-3, 6-4-3, 5-3, 3-6-3, and slow rollers to 3B, SS, 2B and 3-5 play. Screen must be removed for 3-6-3 drills.

Fungo hitters must wait for each other's grounders to pass the alternate fielder. Once timing is aligned for fungo hitters, many grounders can be fielded in a short period of time. In all, this series of drills can be completed within 20 minutes.

Pitcher's Fielding Drills

The entire pitching staff and catching corps work on these drills at least twice a week during the fall and early spring. By improving their fielding fundamentals, our pitchers can field their position batter, helping themselves, their infielders, and the team.

Divide the pitchers into two groups, with one group on the mound and the other at first base. The two groups rotate after each play.

Drill No. 1 — Covering 1B
Pitcher tosses ball to catcher, Coach hits fungo to pitcher-first baseman, who tosses ball underhand to pitcher running up the line covering 1B. Should grounder be bobbled, pitcher sets up as first baseman for the throw.

Drill No. 2 — Comebacker with throw to 2B
Pitcher tosses ball to catcher. Coach hits fungo to pitcher who fields ball, turns and, using proper footwork (crow hop), throws to pitcher-second baseman for 1-4-3 double play.

Drill No. 3 — Comebacker with throw to SS.
Same as Drill No. 2 except that pichers will field throws from shortstop side for 1-6-3 double play.

Drill No. 4 — Combacker and holding runner at 2B.
Pitching from stretch with runner at 2B, pitcher tosses ball to catcher. Coach hits fungo to pitcher who fields ball, checks runner at 2B, then throws to 1B.

Drill No. 5 — Comebacker and holding runner at 3B.
Same as drill No. 4, but checking runner at 3B before throw to 1B.

Drill No. 6 — Fielding bunts with runners on 1B, 2 B, or 1B and 2B.
Pitching from stretch with runner at 1B, pitcher tosses ball to catcher. Coach rolls out bunt. Pitcher fields bunt and throws to 1B, again using proper footwork. Should ball be bunted hard or popped up, pitcher could throw to 2B for force out.

With runners at 1B and 2B, same action, but throw to 3B if bunt is too hard or popped up.

Drill No. 7 — Covering home on passed ball/wild pitch.
Pitcher tosses ball to catcher, who in turn rolls ball toward backstop. Pitcher runs in to cover home plate as catcher retrieves ball and throws to pitcher covering the plate. Different angles should be made by catcher in rolling ball.

Drill No. 8 — Intentional Pass, Pitch Outs and Squeeze Break-Ups.
Pitchers line up in three groups at mound and toss to three catchers

lined up across home plate. After three or four intentional passes, practice pitch outs to left- and right-handed batters. Then work on breaking up squeeze attempts.

For breaking up attempted squeeze, pitchers form one line at mound and another at 3B. Pitching from stretch, pitcher checks runner at 3B and begins wind-up. If runner does not break for home, pitcher throws curve ball. If runner breaks, pitcher changes to fast ball and pitches out to catcher.

This series of drills takes up to 45 minutes to work but can be reduced to 20-30 minutes. It is designed for 9 to 12 pitchers and 3 catchers. Catchers should wear full set of equipment.

Additional Facts on Hitting, Pitching and Defensive Positions

Baseball Tips:

1. Keep eyes on the ball and mind on the game.
2. Practice batting — runs win baseball games.
3. Be alert to signals — missing one could lose a game.
4. Always run out an "easy chance" — anything can happen.
5. Teamwork is key to success. If it's good for the team, it's good for you.

Hitting

At times the long ball hitter proves to be the "star" of a game, but the player who consistently punches out singles and doubles provides the real basis for team success. So often, hitters lacking great physical strength "swing from the heels" in attempting to become sluggers. A well-laced surprise bunt, a high bouncing infield hit or a smash through the infield pays off in game-winning runs.

A batter should maintain balance and be ready to meet the ball squarely. Often a shorter stride provides for better body control. Good eye contact is a must along with hitting the ball in front of the body with a level swing.

To be a truly good hitter, a batter must learn to hit all types of pitches. Once the opposing pitcher learns that a batter can hit only fast balls, the pitcher is certain to throw that batter curves, drops and other breaking pitches.

Pitching

Ability and control are a pitcher's prime assets. Neither is much good without the other, and both are useless without practice.

A pitcher should develop a good assortment of breaking pitches to complement a strong fast ball. For the most part, breaking pitches should be kept low. Some pitchers develop a rising fast ball or an off speed pitch effective at shoulder height. The ability to vary the speed of each pitch is another important asset, one which can be acquired through dedication and practice.

A pitcher has an important role as a defensive infielder. Many games have been won through the pitcher's fielding ability as well as his pitching talent. To be successful, a pitcher must back up plays and cover bases when necessary.

Physical conditioning is important to a pitcher as in the case of any athlete. Most managers and coaches prescribe running drills to keep pitchers' legs in shape. Strength and endurance to pitch for seven innings or longer are required.

The Catcher

As a workhorse of the ball club, the catcher instills confidence in the pitcher and guides him and other teammates on the field.

His job requires studying opposing batters so as to call pitches which capitalize on the batters' weaknesses. Because of his commanding position behind the plate, the good catcher encourages his teammates, keeps them hustling and makes sure they are in position to play the batter properly.

The experienced catcher blocks pitches, throws off his mask quickly to catch pop flies and guards the plate forcing the runner to run into the tag. A good receiver is relaxed and in command of his emotions at all times.

The First Baseman

The first base position is one of the busiest in the lineup and involves more than being able to catch and hold a thrown ball. Either in a direct or assisting role, the first baseman is involved with almost every play. He must know how to handle bunts, when and how to throw the ball and back-up throws to home plate, how to take a relay from the outfield, when to hold the runner on first base and many other phases of the game.

A good first baseman moves around and shifts his position when necessary. Touching the bag when taking the throw is a mechanical action which should become second nature. While many short players have become good first basemen, the taller player has a reach advantage important to playing the position well. The left-handed player also has an advantage in that he can throw to other bases more easily.

One further point: the successful first baseman catches the ball with both hands when possible. He saves the spectacular one-hand grab until the time it really counts.

The Second Baseman

With many baseball teams relying on left-handed hitters, the second baseman gets his share of action.

Often, second base is a pivot position for double plays. A second baseman shifts his feet quickly and throws accurately. Speed and timing are key factors to a successful double play.

Also, a second baseman should keep in mind these vital points:

1. Charge slowly hit ground balls and snap throws to first base. Keep eyes on erratic bouncing grounders. Knock down tough chances, recover and throw the runner out.

2. Back up teammates and hustle out to take the throw from outfielders. Know where to make the relay throw and throw accurately.

3. Coordinate with the shortstop as to who will cover second base to cut down an attempted steal.

4. Practice fielding "Texas League" pop flies and whirling to make the throw back to the infield after the catch.

5. Drill with the first baseman to strengthen the defense of the infielder's right side.

The Third Baseman

The third baseman is keeper of the infield's "hot corner." He must handle everything from sizzling line drives or one-hop shots to slowly rolling bunts. Above all he must keep his mind on the game so as to anticipate the next play.

A third baseman's most important physical asset is his ability to field a ball and throw to first base in one motion.

Runners on first and second bases put great pressure on the third baseman to think and act quickly. Often, he must range far to the left to make the play in front of the shortstop, back up teammates and take throws for plays at third base.

The third baseman should position himself after making these assessments:

1. Is the batter right- or left-handed?

2. Is he a fast baserunner?

3. Does the situation call for a sacrifice, a squeeze play or a drag bunt?

4. Does defense strategy call for a double play attempt, a force on the lead runner or a play at home plate?

The Shortstop

Because he must cover so much area and participate in such a wide variety of plays, the shortstop position is considered most often as the most demanding within the infield.

Without hesitation, the shortstop must react to any situation — run back quickly for pop flies, charge slowly hit grounders, make strong, accurate throws to first base from deep in the "hole" as well as many other plays.

The shortstop should always play the ball and not wait for the ball to play him. Hard smashes have to be handled as best they can be, yet often a quick recovery and good throw retire the runner.

The shortstop should keep these points in mind also:

1. On a double play, throw chest-high to the second baseman.

2. As a pivot man on the double play, tag the base with either foot according to the circumstances of the play.

3. With runners on base, be alert to possibilities of making a relay throw from the outfield or cutting off throws within the infield.

4. Do not fight the ball. Make the fielding plays with a relaxed, fluid motion.

The Outfielders

The outfielder must always be alert as to what to do with the ball, should the ball come to him. He should be mindful of the game situation at all times.

A moment's delay may permit a runner to take another base, or worse yet, score the game-winning run. An outfielder also should note these factors:

1. To gain the opponents' respect, develop a strong, accurate throwing arm. Keep the trajectory of the throw low to the ground. On throws to home plate, aim for the pitching mound and bounce the throw into the plate.

2. To avoid costly collisions with fellow outfielders, always call for fly balls.

3. Block grounds balls in the outfield. Make sure the ball doesn't get through.

4. Always throw ahead of the runner.

5. Back up teammates and avoid spectacular, one-hand grabs unless necessary.

Glossary of Baseball Terms

ABOARD: A player on base is said to be "aboard."

ARBITER: An umpire.

ASSIST: A fielding credit earned by a player who helps a teammate make a put-out. Should the teammate fail to make the put-out because of a misplay, the first player is still given credit for an assist.

AWAY: The number of outs, such as "one away" instead of "one out."

BACKSTOP: While a catcher is often called "the backstop," the term is more often applied to the fencing behind the plate.

BACK UP: To take a position to the rear of a teammate to retrieve any balls which the teammate might fail to catch.

BAG: A base. Also called "sack," "hassock," "pillow," "canvas," etc.

BALK: Making a motion to pitch without immediately delivering the ball to the batter.

BALL: Today's baseball is composed of a cork or rubber center with a tight wool winding and horsehide cover. Check league rules regarding size and weight requirements.

"BALL": The term applied to a pitched ball which does not enter the batter's strike zone, and which the batter does not attempt to hit with his bat. (See "Base on Balls.")

BASE: The four "stations" on a ballfield which runners on the offensive team must touch in succession before scoring — first base, second base, third base and home base known as home plate.

BASE HIT: A batted ball which allows the batter to reach a base safely, provided that he does not reach first base through a fielding error or a fielder's choice and provided that no other runner is forced out.

BASELINE: A more-or-less imaginary space, six feet wide, within which a runner must stay while running bases. If the runner flagrantly moves outside of this lane, he can be called out unless he is trying to avoid a fielder who is attempting to catch a batted ball.

BASE ON BALLS: The penalty imposed on a pitcher who delivers four "balls" to a batter. The batter is allowed to go to first base.

BASES FULL: Baserunners on first, second and third base. Also known as "bases loaded," "bases jammed," "three men on," etc.

BAT: A regulation baseball bat must be of one-piece wood or approved material. Bats are constructed of a variety of lengths and weights. Check your league rules for size and weight requirements.

BATTER'S BOX: The area in which the batter must stand. There is a batter's box on each side of home plate. Each is six feet long and four feet wide, and is placed six inches from home plate.

BATTERY: The combination of the pitcher and the catcher.

BATTING AVERAGE: The number of hits divided by the number of times at bat. The result is usually expressed in three decimals.

BATTING ORDER: The order in which players take their turn at bat. It is set before the game begins, and cannot be changed during play. however, player substitutes can be made.

BEAT OUT: To hit a ball to an infielder and reach first base ahead of that fielder's throw, for a hit.

BLEEDER: A batted ball which just trickles past the defensive players for a "weak" base hit.

BLOOPER: A batted ball which arches over the heads of the infielders and drops in front of the outfielders for a base hit.

BOBBLE: Juggling the ball while attempting a catch, or dropping the ball for an error.

BOTTOM: The second part of an inning. For instance, the second half of the fourth inning is known as the "bottom" of the fourth. The first part of an inning is known as the "top."

BOX SCORE: A description of the events of a game kept in condensed form by the use of certain symbols for the various types of possible plays.

BUNT: A ball tapped by a batter to roll slowly out into the infield. Bunts are usually attempted in an effort to advance another baserunner, but they are also used to allow the batter to reach first base safely by catching the defensive team off guard.

CATCHER: The defensive player who stands behing home plate to receive balls thrown by the pitcher.

CENTER FIELDER: The defensive player who guards center field, the outfield area beyond second base.

CHANGE-OF-PACE: A pitcher's ability to vary the speed of his delivery of pitches, thus confusing the batter.

CHEST PROTECTOR: A device used by a catcher or a plate umpire to keep hard-thrown or hard-hit balls from causing injury.

CHOKE: To grip a baseball bat more closely to the "trademark" than is usual. "Choking the bat" is often done to gain accuracy in hitting the ball.

CIRCUIT CLOUT: A home run. Batter circles all four bases.

CLEAN THE BASES: To hit a home run with players on base, thus clearing all the bases of runners.

CLEAN-UP: To hit a home run with players on base, thus clearing all the bases of runners.

COACH: A member of the team who stands near either first or third base to give baserunning instructions to the team's players.

COMPLIMENTARY RUNNER: A substitute baserunner, who by mutual consent of the opposing coaches or managers does not prevent the original runner from remaining in the game.

CORNER: Portions of home plate; the part of the plate closest to a batter is known as "the inside corner." The part furthermost from him is known as "the outside corner." The other bases are known as "the initial corner" (first base), the "keystone corner" (second base), and the "hot corner" (third base).

COUNT: The number of balls and strikes on a batter. A count of "1 and 2" means that the batter has one ball and two strikes on him.

COUNTER: A run. Also "tally," "marker."

CROWDING THE PLATE: A batter moving close to the plate and refusing to back away with the pitch.

CURVE: A ball pitched with spin to move in a curve rather than a straight path.

CUT: To swing at a pitched ball. Also, a ball which passes over a corner of home plate is said to "cut the corner" for a strike.

CUT-OFF: To intercept a ball thrown to another teammate. A fielder will often cut off a throw aimed at homeplate to trap a player running to another base.

DEAD BALL: A ball no longer in play.

DEEP: A defensive player who stands some distance beyond his usual playing position is said to be playing "deep." Opposite of "shallow."

DELAYED STEAL: An attempt to steal a base whereby the runner does not start his dash until the usual moment for attempting the steal has passed. (See Steal).

DELIVER: To pitch the ball.

DIAMOND: The area formed by the four bases.

DIE: To be stranded on a base as the third out is made.

DOUBLE: A base hit on which the batter is able to reach second base safely despite errorless fielding by the defensive team.

DOUBLE PLAY: Two consecutive put-outs made between the time the pitcher delivered the ball to the batter and the time the ball is returned to him again in the pitcher's box. Also called "twin-killing."

DOUBLE STEAL: A "double steal" occurs when two runner steal bases on the same play.

DOWN: Denotes outs. "Two Down" means that there are two outs.

DRIVE: A hard-hit ball which travels in a fairly straight line.

DROP: A type of pitch in which the ball drops downward as it nears or crosses the plate.

EARNED RUN: A run which was scored through offensive play rather than through a defensive error.

EARNED RUN AVERAGE: The average number of earned runs which a pitcher allows during a full game. To find the earned run average, divide the number of earned runs allowed by the number of innings pitched and multiply by nine.

ERROR: Any defensive misplay which allows a batter to remain at bat longer than he should, or a baserunner to remain on base longer than he should,, or a runner to reach base or take an extra base. However, a base on balls is not an error, nor is a wild pitch or a passed ball.

EXTRA-BASE HIT: A base hit on which the batter gets more than one base.

FAIR BALL: Any legally batted ball which is touched or which stops in fair territory between home plate and first base or home plate and third base; or which lands inside either foul line when bouncing past first or third base; or which first hits on or inside either foul line on a fly past the infield.

FIELDER'S CHOICE: A play in which a fielder, after taking a batted ball, elects to make a play on a baserunner rather than on the batter.

FIELDING AVERAGE: To find a fielder's defensive average, add his toatal fielding chances (put-outs, assist and errors) and divide this number into the total of his put-outs and assists.

FIRST BASE: The base to which the batter runs after hitting the ball. It is 90 feet from homeplate, along the right-field foul line.

FIRST BASEMAN: The defensive player who covers the territory around first base and who generally retires a large number of batters by receiving the throws of the other infielders after the batter has hit a ground ball.

FLY: A ball that is hit into the air, usually to the outfield.

FORCE OUT: An out occurring when a defensive player in possession of the ball touches any base before a runner who must reach that base touches the base. Thus, the ordinary out at first base is a force out. However, the term is usually applied to situations in which there are runners on base before the batter hits the ball Force outs can ocur at any of the four bases.

FORFEIT: An umpire may forfeit any game and award it to one team for a variety of reasons, such as delay of game, refusal to continue play, rule violations, etc. The score of a forfeited game is 9-0 in favor of the team not at fault.

FOUL BALL: A batted ball which is touched or stops outside of the foul line between home plate and first or third base; which bounces past first or third base in foul territory, or which first lands outside the foul lines on a fly ball past first or third base. A foul caught on the fly is an out for the batter. The first two foul hits in a time at bat count as strikes; succeeding ones do not. However, a foul bunt attempt after two strikes is an out for the batter.

FOUL LINE: A three-inch white line extending from home plate out to the boundaries of the playing field. The two foul lines form right angles at home plate. The foul line itself is considered fair territory.

FOUL TIP: A foul ball caught by the catcher immediately after leaving the hitter's bat on a direct line into the catcher's hand. Any foul tip is a strike and the ball remains in play.

FULL COUNT: A count of three balls and two strikes on the batter.

FUNGO: A high fly, usually hit by tossing the ball from the hand and then hitting it, to give the fielders practice.

GAME: A game consists of nine innings. The team which has scored the most runs at the end of that time wins the game, unless tied, in which case the game goes into extra innings. If the team batting in the bottom half of each inning scores more runs in eight than the team batting in the top half of the inning scores in nine turns at bat, the game ends without having to play the last half of the ninth inning.

GRAND SLAM: A home run with the bases loaded.

GRASS CUTTER: A sharply hit ball which skims across the top of the grass.

GROOVE: To pitch the ball right in the middle of the strike zone.

GROUNDER: A "grounder" or "ground ball" is a batted ball which hits the ground as soon as it leaves the player's bat and bounces in the infield as it moves toward the outfield.

HIGH: A pitched ball which passes the plate above the strike zone.

HIT: To take one's turn at bat. Also, to make a base hit.

HIT-AND-RUN: An offensive play in which a baserunner begins running as soon as the pitcher starts his delivery. The batter than attempts to hit the ball, often through a spot vacated by the shortstop or second baseman. Often used as a device for avoiding double plays.

HIT BATSMAN: A batter who is hit by a pitched ball. The batter is entitled to move to first base. However, he must make an attempt to get out of the path of the ball.

HIT THE DIRT: To slide.

HOLE: An area not covered by a defensive player. Fielders often shift position against certain batters, leaving large "holes" open which normally don't exist.

HOMER: Short for "Home Run." A base hit whereby the batter runs all the bases and scores a run. Most home runs result from balls hit over the outfield fences. Some result from fast baserunning following a ball hit well out of outfielders' reach, but within the playing area.

HOOK SLIDE: A baserunning maneuver in which the runner, trying to reach a base on a close play, slides feet first into the base and twists his body away from defensive player to touch the base with his rear foot.

INFIELD: Generally, that fair territory bounded by and including the basepaths.

INFIELD HIT: A base hit which does not go past the infielders to the outfield.

INNING: A division of a game. An inning is divided into two halves. A team is allowed to bat during one half of each inning. Since each is allowed three outs, there are six outs per inning.

INSIDE: A pitch which misses the plate on the side closest to the batter.

LAY ONE DOWN: To bunt to ball.

LEAD: A baserunner "takes a lead" when he moves off a base in an effort to put himself closer to the next base. His "lead" cannot be too great, or he may be tagged out.

LEAD-OFF: The player who first bats for his team either in the regular batting order or at the beginning of an inning.

LEFT FIELDER: The defensive player who covers the outfield area beyond third base and shortstop.

LINE DRIVE: A ball batted sharply to travel in a fairly straight line. Also a "clothesliner."

LOSING PITCHING: The pitcher who is charged with the loss if his team is defeated.

MASK: A device worn by catchers and umpires to protect their faces against injury from a batted or thrown ball.

MIX UP: To vary the type and speed of pitches.

MOVE UP: To advance to the next base.

MUFF: To drop a ball.

NO-HITTER: A game in which the pitcher does not give up a single hit, and usually no runs. A "perfect game" is one in which no opponent reaches first base on a hit, error, walk, etc.

ONE-TWO-THREE: Side retired without a batter reaching first base.

OUT: An "out" is the retirement of a batter or baserunner during play. The ways in which a batter or baserunner may be put out are numerous. Each team is allowed three outs during its time at bat in any one inning.

OUTFIELD: In general, the fair territory beyond the infield.

OUTSIDE: A pitched ball which misses the strike zone on the side of the plate furthermost from the batter.

OVER-RUN: To run past a base or to slide past (over-slide) a base placing the runner in danger of being tagged out. However, the batter may overrun first base while attempting to reach there after hitting the ball.

PASSED BALL: A legaly pitched ball which the catcher fails to hold and control provided that the bat did not strike the ball.

PICK OFF: To trap a runner off base with a sudden throw and tag him out.

PINCH HITTER: A player who is sent into the game to bat in place of another player.

PITCHER'S BOX: The place from which the pitcher delivers the ball. In the pitcher's box is the "rubber" or pitcher's plate, a rubber or wood block set flush with the ground. This "rubber" is 60'6'' from the far corner of home plate.

PITCHOUT: A pitch purposely thrown wide of the plat to allow the catcher easier access to the ball. Used to stop a possible steal or hit-and-run.

POP-UP: A short, high fly in or near the infield which can be easily caught.

PUT-OUT: The retiring of a batter or baserunner.

RELAY: To return the ball fromt he outfield to the infield by using several short, fast throws rather than one long (and necessarily slower) throw. For most relays, an infielder moves out into the outfield, takes the throw from the outfielder, and in turn throws it to another infielder.

RIGHT FIELDER: The defensive player who covers the outfield area beyond first base and second base.

RUN: A unit of scoring. A run is scored when a runner touches home plate, having previously touched first second and third bases. The run is counted provided the runner is not forced out, tagged out or the batter is retired for the third out of the inning.

RUNS BATTED IN (RBI): A batter is credited with batting in a run when a baserunner scores when he makes a base hit, a sacrifice, forces in a run by walking or hits into a put-out.

SACRIFICE: An advancement of a baserunner by the batter who deliberately hits the ball in such a way that the defensive fielders can only make a play on the batter.

SCRATCH HIT: A ball, usually weakly hit, which none of the fielders can reach in time to retire the batter.

SECOND BASE: The next base after first base. It is the only base not touching the foul lines.

SECOND BASEMAN: The defensive player who generally covers second base and the area to the first base side of second.

SHORTSTOP: A defensive player who generally covers second base and the area to the third base side of second.

SHUT OUT: To prevent the opposing team from scoring a run.

SINGLE: A base hit on which the batter reaches and stops on first base.

SLIDE: Sliding along the ground toward the base to avoid being put out.

SQUEEZE: Advancing a runner from third to home plate by bunting the ball. The baserunner starts runing as soon as the ball is pitched. If the batter hits the ball properly, the defensive team has very little time to retire the runner.

STEAL: To advance to another base on the strength of baserunning alone. A runner may steal any base but first.

STRAIGHTAWAY: The term used to describe the normal defensive position of a team, wherein each player remains in his usual fielding area rather than shifting to the right or to the left.

STRIKE: A penalty imposed on the bater for either failing to hit a ball which enters the strike zone; or swinging at any pitchand missing it; or hitting a foul ball which is not caught on the fly. In the latter case, if two strikes are on the batter, a foul ball does not count as another strike. If a batter with two strikes bunts a foul ball, he is out. The strike zone is ordinarily described as that area bounded by the sides of home plate and the batter's shoulders and knees.

TAG UP: The action of a baserunner is touching a base while a fielder is catching a fly ball. The runner must do so if he desires to advance to the next base without danger of being put out at the base from which he leaves. If he leaves this base before a fielder catches the ball, he can be put out providing a defensive player touches this base with the ball in his possession before the runner returns to tag the base.

TEXAS LEAGUER: A weakly-hit fly ball which arches over the heads of the infielders and drops in front of the outfielders for a base hit.

THIRD BASE: The next base after second base, its outside edge touches the left field foul line. Next stop — home plate!

THIRD BASEMAN: The defensive player who covers the area around third base.

TOP: To hit the top portion of the ball so that the ball bounces downward sharply, resulting in a weak ground ball.

TRAP: To catch a ball immediately after it has taken its first bounce.

TRIPLE: To make a three-base hit.

TRIPLE PLAY: The retirement of three offensive players between the time a ball leaves the pitcher's hand and is returned to him in the pitcher's box. It can only occur with at least two runners on base and no one out, hence is rare.

WAIT OUT: An offensive strategy by a batter who refuses to swing at the pitcher's throw until he either gets a base hit or makes the pitcher throw a good ball to hit.

WALK: A base on balls. Also called a "pass," a "free-ticket," a "gift," etc.

WILD PITCH: An inaccurately delivered pitch which the catcher has little or no chance of stopping or holding. It is not counted as such unless the throw permits the batter to reach first base or a baserunner advances.